First Facts™

From Farm to Table

From Apples
to Applesauce

by Kristin Thoennes Keller

Consultant:
Denise Yockey, Executive Director
Michigan Apple Committee
Lansing, Michigan

Capstone
press

Mankato, Minnesota

First Facts is published by Capstone Press
151 Good Counsel Drive, P.O. Box 669, Mankato, Minnesota 56002
www.capstonepress.com

Library of Congress Cataloging-in-Publication Data
Thoennes Keller, Kristin.
    From apples to applesauce / by Kristin Thoennes Keller.
    p. cm.—(First facts. From farm to table)
    Includes bibliographical references and index.
    ISBN 0-7368-2633-5 (hardcover)
    1. Applesauce—Juvenile literature. 2. Apples—Juvenile literature. [1. Applesauce. 2. Apples.]
I. Title. II. Series.
TP441.A6T46 2005
641.6'411—dc22   2003023370

Summary: An introduction to the basic concepts of food production, distribution, and consumption
    by tracing the production of applesauce from apples to the finished product.

Editorial Credits
Roberta Schmidt, editor; Jennifer Bergstrom, designer; Kelly Garvin, photo researcher; Eric Kudalis,
    product planning editor

Photo Credits
Capstone Press/Gary Sundermeyer, front cover, 5 (foreground), 6–7, 8–9, 10–11, 19
Ingram Publishing, back cover
John Marshall Photography, 14, 20
Leahy Orchards Inc., 12–13, 15, 16–17
PhotoDisc Inc., 1

Artistic Effects
PhotoDisc Inc., 5 (background)

1 2 3 4 5 6   09 08 07 06 05 04

Table of Contents

Eating Apples with a Spoon

Applesauce is a healthy food that people eat with a spoon. Some kinds of applesauce are smooth like pudding. Other kinds of applesauce are chunky.

Applesauce has to be made before people can eat it. Making applesauce takes many steps.

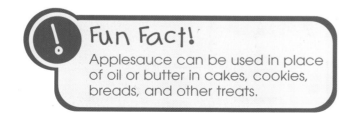

Fun Fact!
Applesauce can be used in place of oil or butter in cakes, cookies, breads, and other treats.

Amazing Apples

Applesauce is made from apples. Apples grow on trees. Most apple trees grow in places that have cold winters. The cold weather helps the trees get ready to make apples in the spring. Many apple trees grow on farms called apple **orchards**.

! Fun Fact!
There are 7,500 kinds of apples grown in the world.

Picking Apples

Most apples are ready to pick at the end of summer or the start of fall. Workers often climb ladders to pick the apples. They put the apples in bags. When a bag is full, workers gently dump the apples into a box.

Fun Fact!
Some full-grown apples are the size of an eyeball. Other kinds of apples are almost as large as a baby's head.

9

Packing Apples

After the apples are picked, they are kept in cool rooms. The cool air keeps the apples fresh until they are packed.

Workers and machines wash and sort the apples. The apples are put into boxes and bags.

Fun Fact!
In colonial times, some people called apples "winter bananas."

To the Factory

Some apples are sold to large companies. These companies use apples to make juice, applesauce, and other foods. Workers load the apples onto trucks. The trucks take the apples to **factories**.

Fun Fact!
The average person in the United States eats about 45 pounds (20 kilograms) of apples and apple products each year.

13

Making Applesauce

At the factories, the apples ride on a moving belt. The belt takes the apples through water. When the fruit is clean, it is ready to be made into applesauce.

14

Machines remove the skin, **core**, and seeds. Then, the apples are chopped into pieces and cooked. Sugar and flavors sometimes are added.

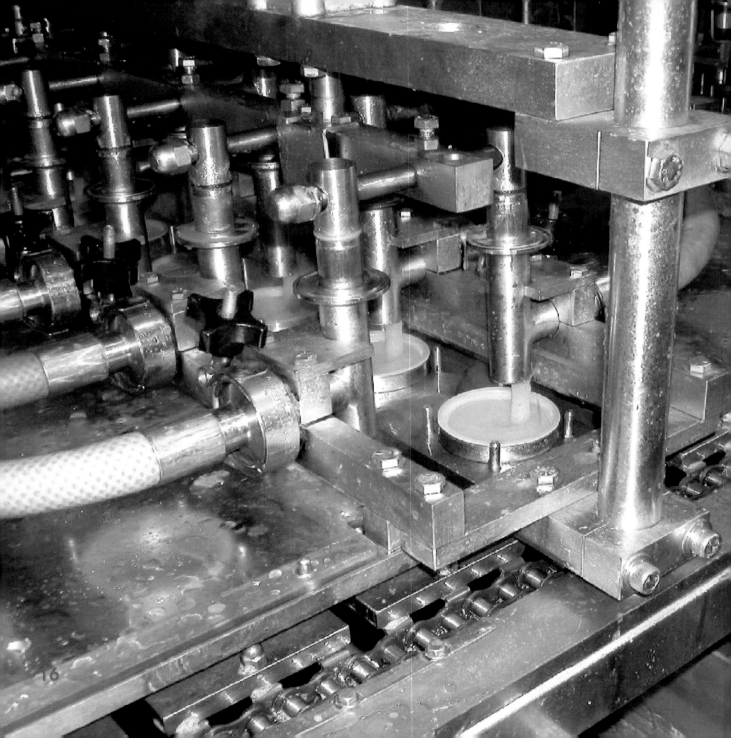

To the Store

Machines squirt the hot applesauce into new cans, jars, or cups. Then, these **containers** are **sealed**.

Companies sell the applesauce to stores. Workers put the applesauce in trucks or on trains for the trip to the stores.

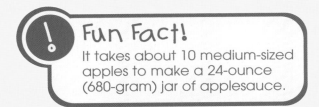

Fun Fact!
It takes about 10 medium-sized apples to make a 24-ounce (680-gram) jar of applesauce.

Where to Find Applesauce

Applesauce can be found at almost every grocery store. Apple orchards sometimes also sell applesauce. Some people make applesauce at home on the stove. No matter how it's made, applesauce is a sweet, fruity treat that is good to eat.

Fun Fact!
Applesauce was the first food eaten in space. In 1962, astronaut John Glenn ate applesauce from a tube while he went around Earth in a spacecraft.

Most apple trees do not come from apple seeds. Apple growers use a process called grafting to grow new apple trees. A grower puts branches from one apple tree onto the stump of another apple tree. The grower tapes the parts together. The parts grow together to make a new tree.

Hands On: Homemade Applesauce

You can make your own applesauce at home. Ask an adult to help you.

What You Need

apple peeler

knife

4 medium-sized apples

large saucepan

liquid measuring cup

½ cup (120 mL) water

spoon

dry-ingredient measuring cup

¼ cup (60 mL) sugar

cinnamon

What You Do

1. Peel, core, and slice the apples. Cut the apple slices into small chunks.
2. Put the apples in a pan with the water. Simmer for about 15 minutes over medium heat.
3. Stir in the sugar and a sprinkle of cinnamon.
4. Wait until the applesauce cools. Eat the applesauce warm, or refrigerate it and eat it cold.

Glossary

container (kuhn-TAYN-er)—a holder

core (KOR)—the hard center of an apple that contains seeds

factory (FAK-tuh-ree)—a building where products are made in large numbers; factories often use machines to make products.

orchard (OR-churd)—a farm where fruit trees grow

seal (SEEL)—to close something up

Read More

Mayo, Gretchen Will. *Applesauce.* Where Does Our Food Come From? Milwaukee: Weekly Reader Early Learning Library, 2004.

Mayr, Diane. *Out and About at the Apple Orchard.* Field Trips. Minneapolis: Picture Window Books, 2003.

Robbins, Ken. *Apples.* New York: Atheneum Books for Young Readers, 2002.

Internet Sites

FactHound offers a safe, fun way to find Internet sites related to this book. All of the sites on FactHound have been researched by our staff.

Here's how:
1. Visit *www.facthound.com*
2. Type in this special code **0736826335** for age-appropriate sites. Or enter a search word related to this book for a more general search.
3. Click on the **Fetch It** button.

FactHound will fetch the best sites for you!

Index